Totally Girls

Ready To Wear

Phidal

Come join the fun and read about all kinds of great activities.
This sticker book is for girls only! You can place
the reusable stickers anywhere you like.
After completing all the games, use the last
page to create a story of your own.

5 years and up.

©2004 Phidal Publishing Inc.
Produced and Published by Phidal Publishing Inc.
5740 Ferrier, Montreal, Quebec, Canada H4P 1M7
All rights reserved.
Printed in Italy.
www.phidal.com

ISBN: 2-7643-0187-1

We acknowledge the financial support of the government of Canada
through the BPIDP for our publishing activities.

Stylin' Seasons

A true fashion pro looks great in any kind of weather. Use your stickers to match each girl to the season she's dressed for.

Winter

Spring

Summer

Fall

Weather Match-up

A change in the weather is a great excuse to go shopping for new clothes! Match your clothing stickers to the girls who are wearing them!

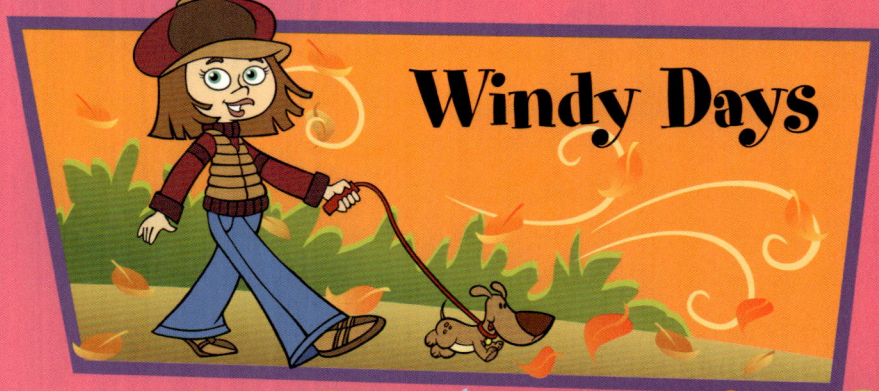

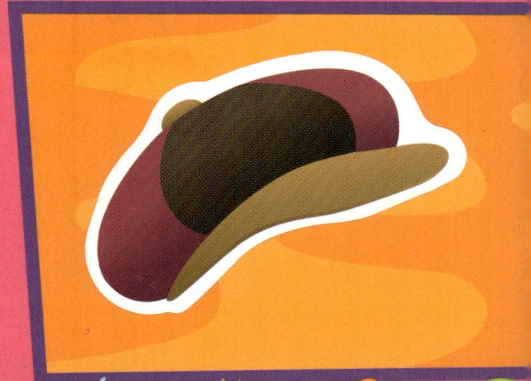

Cold Days

Warm Days

Rainy Days

Windy Days

Having a Beach Blast!

This busy beach is the best place to hang out with friends on warm sunny days.
Decorate this awesome summertime scene with your stickers.

Winter Wonderland

Brenda and Andrea love to skate, but it looks like they're missing a few important things. Use your stickers to help them dress warmly for the winter season.

Wild Weather!

These girls may live far away from each other, but they all share a great sense of style. Match the weather conditions in each area with the girl who's best dressed for it.

Snow

Rain

Breezy

Sunny

Partly Cloudy

Fit and Fun!

Being outdoors is fun anytime of the year, and these girls always do it in style. Use your stickers to match each girl to the activity she's dressed for!

Skiing

Snowboarding

Jumping in Puddles

Gardening

Picking Apples

Hiking

Walking the Dog

Diving

Rollerblading

Building Snowmen

What's Missing?

School is the best place to show off your fantastic wardrobe. Make sure the bottom scene looks like the top by adding the missing girls and objects with your stickers.